THE ABSTRACT FIGURE:

CAROL KREEGER DAVIDSON

A RETROSPECTIVE

WITH ESSAYS BY

ROBERT P. METZGER

DONALD KUSPIT

CYNTHIA NADELMAN

SALLY FISHER

PHOTOGRAPHY BY

JERRY L. THOMPSON

E. IRVING BLOMSTRANN

AND OTHERS

READING PUBLIC MUSEUM   READING, PENNSYLVANIA

Published in conjunction with a traveling exhibition, 2002–2003
at the following institutions:

READING PUBLIC MUSEUM
Reading, Pennsylvania

THE NATIONAL MUSEUM OF WOMEN IN THE ARTS
Washington, D.C.

NEW BRITAIN MUSEUM OF AMERICAN ART
New Britain, Connecticut

Library of Congress Control Number: 2002 141063
ISBN Hardcover: 0-965494-3-8
Softcover: 0-965494-4-6

Front cover illustration:
Designated Angels. 1996
Aluminum, acrylic
Large figures: 73 x 15 x 23 inches
Smaller figure: 56 x 9 x 18 inches
Smallest figure: 24 x 19 x 38 inches

Back cover illustration:
Designated Angels (detail)

Designed by Bethany Johns
Edited and produced by Sally Fisher
Printed and bound by Toppan Printing Company, Tokyo, Japan

CONTENTS

INTRODUCTION

The sculpture of Carol Kreeger Davidson is confrontational and direct. Never passive, her off-the-pedestal, close-to-lifesize images are sometimes bold and brash, possessing a Yankee exuberance and vitality seldom matched in the work of her peers. Over the past three decades, Davidson has created a large group of works that have broadened the formal language of geometric sculpture with their groundbreaking use of industrial materials to reinvent and reaccess the human form.

The use of these mundane materials themselves—the ordinary "stuff" of consumer society—was certainly not new to twentieth-century sculpture. Rather, it is Davidson's relentless experimentation with new working methods and her extraordinary range and respect for the materials—metal (especially aluminum sheets), fiberglass-paper (laminated to canvas or linen), wood, neoprene, urethane, rope, cable, and Arches Cover paper, in various juxtapositions—which make her forms so mysterious, haunting, and unforgettable.

Davidson's breakthrough technique of bending, folding, and bolting rather than welding sets up an integration of oppositions. She has taken the method of paper collage and applied it to an unlikely material with astonishing results. Her use of color is unparalleled in contemporary sculpture. The nonhuman tonal relationships, which cover nascent human form, stir ambiguous emotional tensions. Davidson's predilection for audacious high-keyed color strips derives from her love of Egyptian art.

Each new generation of artists either builds upon or reacts against the work of its immediate predecessors. In comparison with her precursors, Davidson chose to pare down the three-dimensional human figure to a greater extent than did Giacometti, Picasso, Armitage, Moore, Nakian or Lipchitz. Her sculpture references the streamlined effulgence of the machine aesthetic of the early twentieth century, combining aspects of natural forms with mechanical shapes. The tubular, erect figures that she has folded into being are the converse of Henry Moore's languidly reclining figures. Nevertheless, Davidson and Moore do share an affinity for massive dimensions and sensuously finished surfaces that imbue the work of both with a timeless architectonic quality.

In the second half of the twentieth century, as new industrial materials and processes became available, artists responded differently in their ways of depicting the human body. Davidson's persistent preference for these materials, along with her dominant verticality, transposes her images ever closer to the edge of abstraction, her stridently simplified forms eradicating distinctions of detail. Her sculpture presents an ambiguity between the implicit standing human figure and the enfolding garments (robes or cloaks) that drape the body. The rounded, painted sheets of aluminum or bronze are far removed from either drapery or flesh and bone. As often as not, her forms are read as abstractions rather than as human anatomy pulsating with life. Mysterious and impenetrable, they bridge the line between abstraction and realism.

Davidson's decided preference for tubular and columnar shapes, often with overlapping planes delineating sensuous contours, brings these works closer to the architecture of Frank Gehry than to Modernist sculpture of the human figure. Her forms are polar opposites of the sleek elongation of Giacometti or the modular-unit beam constructions of Joel Shapiro. The self-enclosed forms are created by rolling and bending sheets of metal or fiberglass-paper and linen into smooth tubular forms that reveal few anatomical details. When human body parts are referenced, it is usually an arm from the joint of the elbow or the leg below the knee joint. Davidson has mastered the tapering of these limbs, which contract at the top and bottom and become more tumescent as they reach the center of the torso.

Many of Davidson's sculptures are headless, topped with hooded, ribbonlike curved forms. Legs and feet are often suggested by an incised slit in the lower portion of the form. In some works, wide-legged stances indicate aggression or impending action. Human arms and hands are even more problematic to the enfolding vertical metal sheets; when the columns are not armless, these appendages hang at the sides or are enfolded on the upper torso with only the merest hint of hands.

This lack of detail is far from the idealization of the human form that has characterized so much of Western sculpture from the ancient Greeks through Gaston Lachaise. As the Greeks well understood, the rounded vertical column is the ultimate metaphor for the standing human body. Davidson intuitively appreciated the example of the ancients and was challenged by the enormous restrictions and limitations of the rigid columnar form. In terms of anatomy, this format smooths over the convex protuberances and cavities of the human body, so it is often only Davidson's wry allegorical titles with references to literature, history, or anthropology that reveal a human point of departure.

Like the Minimalists, Davidson sometimes eliminates the artist's handprint; but as a Postminimalist, she allows her own vital personality to shine through in her work. Unlike the seminaturalistic images of Henry Moore, her forms are dehumanized by their flattened and rounded materials, though strong emotions always boil just beneath the surface. Despite the viewer's tendency to anthropomorphize vertical forms into anatomical parts, Davidson's sculpture tends to resist direct reference to the human body, even when the wellspring of the underlying idea for it is derived from literature or mythology. The images, often from ancient or primitive sources or both, exist in their own right as industrial objects with scant fidelity to the natural world. Yet they never enter the realm of pure abstraction as do works by David Smith and Anthony Caro.

Davidson's concerns thus have little room for the Western ideals of human beauty but resonate with the powerful totemic spirit of Pacific-Asian art. This determined, tenacious detachment from the notion of idealization actualizes her sculpture as unified solid mass in space. A self-contradictory dichotomy arises out of her antirealism on the one hand and her reluctance to forsake figuration entirely. Davidson's work circling around the theme of the human figure—her quasi realism or stylized figuration of conical and hemispherical elements—forces the viewer to rethink unresolved ideas of human and cosmic form in space.

Davidson's extreme simplification of form brings a remarkable fluidity and elegance to her best work, suggestive of flowing drapery and seamless coverings. The material is antithetical to diaphanous or silken textiles; rather, it appears strong and thick. The enigmas of life and anatomy are thus enfolded within her forms, enhancing them with an impenetrable mystery. Secrets shrouded away from the light of day arouse the imagination, particularly in the female goddesses and earth mothers.

The various elements of Davidson's works are abstracted into simple, harmonious forms with the elimination of anatomical details. In this way Davidson reveals the essence of her subjects rather than their exterior form, leaving the observer free to fill these empty vessels with spatial convolutions of significance and meaning. Davidson's ability to ponder the ambivalence between edge and surface, rigid and flowing forms, abstraction and reality, single forms and clusters, strength and weakness of material, open space and massive blocks, places her work among the most thought-provoking and complex expressions of late-twentieth- and early-twenty-first-century sculpture.

ROBERT P. METZGER, PH.D.
Director Emeritus and Consultant, Art and Art History
Reading Public Museum
Reading, Pennsylvania

FROM POSTMINIMALISM TO TOTEMISM:
Carol Kreeger Davidson's Journey to the Self

DONALD KUSPIT

(1)

"By the end of the sixties," Robert Pincus-Witten writes, in explanation of the rise of Postminimalism, "it was clear that formalist abstraction had been tempered by a new set of formal and moral values, imperatives tempered by despair over the conduct of American politics, (Viet Nam, Watergate, etc.), and energized by the insurgency and success of the women's movement."[1] This certainly fits Carol Kreeger Davidson's sense of the situation and her art. She writes: "For many artists in the mid-seventies, women in particular, concept and process were not enough. For me, content, craft, tension, sensuality and horror of horrors the figure crept unbidden, seeping into the structure I had devised." The formalist abstraction was Minimalism—a very de-energized geometry—and the Postminimalist rebellion against it involved the use of what Pincus-Witten calls "eccentric processes, substances and colorations," all of which were "unacceptable" to Minimalism, especially because they conveyed a sensuality, flexibility, and complex sense of self altogether lacking in its somewhat rigid "formalist sensibility."

Indeed, if, as Pincus-Witten writes, Postminimalism restores the idea of the "uniqueness of personality" that is a "constant value of modern art" but that was lost in Minimalism—if Postminimalism "stresses autobiography, the artistic personal and psyche, stripped bare as it were, layer by layer"—then Kreeger Davidson's sculpture shows the uniqueness of her personality. In a sense, her work is a kind of autobiographical record of the changes wrought in her artistic persona and psyche by the women's movement—by women's new self-consciousness and sense of urgency, issuing in a new sense of personal value. Kreeger Davidson in effect broke free of the male sense of impersonal selfhood implicit in Minimalism even as she used its methods to convey a female sense of personal selfhood. If, as the women's movement declared, "the personal is the political," then Kreeger Davidson's art is socially political to the extent it is personal and aesthetically political to the extent it is "antiformalist," as Pincus-Witten says—to the extent it reminds us that Minimalist formalism, supposedly the climax of modern geometrical art, lacks the human value of modern art.

Kreeger Davidson spent 1967–68 in Borneo as a member of the Peace Corps, a move that suggests her political consciousness. She returned to Borneo in 1982 and

1. Robert Pincus-Witten, *Postminimalism* (New York: Out of London Press, 1977), p. 14.

collaborated on a film called *Borneo Playback; A Sabah Story*, aired by the Public Broadcasting Service in June 1985. It was made "to fulfill a promise to Justin Stimol, a native musician, to tell the story of his people. It was a risk to abandon sculpture for two years, but the human rewards were enormous." Indeed, they filtered into her art, finally informing it completely, adding to its expressive power. Her experience in Borneo is in fact a source of her very personal female totemism. As Kreeger Davidson says, "In knowing the 'other' Asia, I began to know myself." Clearly there is an affiliation and identification with the marginal outside, confirming Kreeger Davidson's sense—woman's sense—of being an outsider herself, in both the art and political worlds, in the seventies.

Perhaps what most disturbed Kreeger Davidson about Minimalism was its emotional sterility—its lack of emotional resonance. It did not speak to women at a time when their emotions ran high, spurring on social and personal revolution in the name of basic human values and rights. The macho implications of Minimalist sculpture were also disturbing. Minimalist geometry tends to dominate space rather than harmonize with it, suggesting the male inability to establish reciprocal relationships. Certainly Minimalist abstraction is beside the point, considering the empathy that Kreeger Davidson felt for the people of Borneo—her expressive alter ego, as it were. In short, Kreeger Davidson's sculpture begins with the Postminimalist rebellion against Minimalist masculinism, hidden behind the facade of its intellectualism, not to say dogmatism. Her art overturns the values of Minimalism to reassert broader modern values, indeed, more deeply human values, that supposedly come "naturally" to women, than the limited ones evident in Minimalism.

Minimalism is generally regarded as the consummate statement of geometrical abstraction, all the more so because from the moment of its first Modernist appearance in Kasimir Malevich's Suprematism it discarded the frame within which the geometrical gestalt was confined. This liberation of the gestalt elevated it into an autonomous construction—unequivocally pure, perfect geometry. Minimalist art lost its subliminal association with the figure (which previous art had retained in the frame, implicitly the window on the world that the traditional painting resembles) and became a symbol of transcendence and intellectual superiority. The imperfect, impure world was replaced by perfect, pure geometry, emblematic of the higher world of the mind—a very Platonic idea. But the transcendental idealism of geometrical autonomy, purity, and perfection was untrue to the reality of women's experience, all the more so because men regarded women's bodies as "impure," their persons as less than perfect, and their autonomy as negligible. Moreover, the hermetic self-sufficiency of the geometrical gestalt seemed to betray the human need for intimacy and self-expression. It seemed to symbolize an authoritarian conception of the male self: the self as dominating rather that giving, indifferent rather than responsive, and in complete control of others as well as itself.

The Minimalist gestalt is a closed system, evoking a inexpressive, remote, static self, more inwardly dead than alive, and in general without any motivating dynamics. Woman's new sense of inner necessity, catalyzed by the women's movement, protested this stultifying "minimal" sense of self, especially because it denied the emotional dialectics of the self. The story of Kreeger Davidson's art is the story of her liberating herself from the restraints of what Lawrence Alloway called Systemic art[2]—a "minimum" art of rules and regulations, forming a procedural system with a predetermined result—while using some of Systemic art's devices to maximize the sense of autonomous female selfhood. She in effect subverts the Minimalist system by appropriating from it what she needs to make clear her feeling of emotional aliveness and female autonomy. She humanizes Minimalism's geometrical gestalt by giving it figurative implications and finally by transforming it into a totemic figure. In her ingenious hands an impersonal abstract form becomes a personal symbol of the elemental female self. Kreeger Davidson's sculpture develops from intellectual and structural autonomy to personal and human autonomy by way of what amounts to a radical feminist critique of Minimalism.

(11)

In a sense, Kreeger Davidson accomplishes what has always been the subliminal goal of modern art, indeed, its project since Paul Cézanne spoke of rendering nature in geometrical form without destroying its vitality: the convincing reconciliation of abstraction and empathy, that is, of inorganic geometry and organic nature. As Wilhelm Worringer suggests, geometrical rationality seems to guarantee survival in the vastness of immeasurable apace, while nature is emotionally nourishing, especially when we identify with its generative power—its fertility. Geometry is inexpressive, nature expressive. To bring together the opposites of the axiomatically inevitable and the dynamically developing is to perform an artistic miracle. To me one of Kreeger Davidson's most important works is *The Big Box, The Bride and Her Husbands, Even,* 1974, a historically as well as personally important Postminimalist work. It effects the reconciliation with innovative brio and marks her feminist as well as artistic rebellion and breakthrough.

The title itself goes against the grain of Marcel Duchamp's famous misogynist work *The Bride Stripped Bare by Her Bachelors, Even, or The Large Glass,* 1915–23, which degrades woman even as it ironically elevates her into a dubious higher realm. In Kreeger Davidson's work, the big box is clearly woman, containing all the substance of life. What is flattened in Duchamp's work is freshly rounded in Kreeger Davidson's work. Indeed, the sculpture is essentially an abstract representation of woman's body as the universal matrix of abundant being. The truly radical—and

2. Lawrence Alloway, "Systemic Painting," in *Minimal Art: A Critical Anthology*, ed. Gregory Battcock (New York: Dutton, 1968), pp. 36–60.

Postminimalist—aspect of Kreeger Davidson's complex sculpture is its use of neoprene, a synthetic rubber. With one material stroke, Kreeger Davidson undermines abstract geometry. The pure becomes impure, the sacred profane—down-to-earth. Rubber is a flexible material, which makes it seem feminine, but it is also dense, durable, and resilient, and as such suggests woman's new ego strength. Kreeger Davidson has reembodied the disembodied geometrical gestalt. She fills the big box with smaller boxes made of neoprene. Thus Kreeger Davidson explodes a symbol of male self-restraint and austerity by her feminine lack of material restraint, for the neoprene boxes bulge—fairly burst—with expressive power. It is implicitly the power of the breast, as the nipple-like forms on the small boxes suggest. Kreeger Davidson has given us a new, Modernist incarnation of the forty-breasted Diana of Ephesus: the Great Goddess, the mother of us all.

Body art emerged decisively during Postminimalism, as Pincus-Witten notes, and Kreeger Davidson's work is a kind of body art. In a sense, it performs the body in symbolic-abstract terms. What also emerges is what Pincus-Witten calls "the 'pictorial/sculptural' mode"—a mixed mode of art making that brings together the expressive possibilities of painting and sculpture. It attempts to combine the intimate textures of painting with the spatial drama of sculpture. At its best, the pictorial/sculptural mode results in a kind of haptic theater, the dramatization of touch and "touching" drama. *The Big Box* is a superb example of haptic theater. Its flexible, fleshlike insides give it a touchy-feely dimension, whereas its box form sets it pristinely apart in space, confirming that it is a space of its own—that woman has her own space ("a room of her own"). The box announces and dramatizes woman's apartness and separateness: her difference. Kreeger Davidson's work is a major contribution to the modernist genre of box sculpture and also to woman's idea of art making, for the smaller boxes are hand-sewn and of quite different sizes, making them intimate and personal. Nonetheless, they all fit together, and there is enough room for them in the large box. There is room for all kinds of beings in the sacred space and sanctuary of the Great Mother. Moreover, the smaller boxes have no fixed place in the big box but can be rearranged, however eccentrically. Thus the sculpture is implicitly "interactive," that is, it invites the viewer's involvement, which makes it all the more intimate, personal, "relational," and female.

(III)

Persephone, 1975, is another neoprene work, with an aluminum plate dividing it in half. This wall sculpture, with its allusion to the daughter of Demeter—she was forced to spend half her time in hell because she had been raped by Hades, thus tasting the forbidden fruit of sex—is already well on the way to what I call Kreeger

Davidson's female totem form, that is, her totemic emblem of female dignity and grace. The aluminum plate is the bright figure on the dark ground of the neoprene sheet; it is an upright, austere figure, set at a right angle to the sheet, as though to sink into and be enveloped by it, thus disappearing into the void. Indeed, the figure seems to be emerging from it and defying that very void. The aluminum plate can be understood as Minimalist, the neoprene sheet makes the work Postminimalist, and its mythological title gives it feminist meaning. *Persephone* is a brilliant example of Kreeger Davidson's mythopoetic imagination at its most aesthetically succinct and a wonderful example of the pictorial/sculptural mode in action.

As early as 1974 Kreeger Davidson was using the geometrical gestalt as a totem form, as *Dance of Life*, 1974, indicates. Four rectangular plates, each stuck in the earth at an angle, tilt away from each other, even as they are held together by cables, which also form rectangular spaces. These "negative" spaces (the rectangular voids) contrast rather starkly with the "positive" spaces (the material rectangles). The tension between the "positive" rectangles is palpable, but so is their unity, however forced it may seem. The work is profoundly self-contradictory, all the more so because it is at odds with the nature in which it is placed. Ostensibly a simple construction, it is in fact dialectically unresolved. A very human situation is suggested: the plates, like human beings, reluctantly but necessarily relate. They must relate if they are not to collapse in a meaningless heap. "In unity there is strength" seems to be the motto of the work, even as disunity is vividly signaled, despite the irony of the unity established by the repetition of the plates and the fact that their measurements are the same. Is Kreeger Davidson commenting on the women's movement, in which people who are fundamentally the same are at odds even as they pursue the same interests?

In his essay on "Systemic Painting," Alloway characterizes Minimalist work as "One-Image art" and writes that "in style analysis we look for unity within variety; in One-Image art we look for variety within conspicuous unity."[3] But in Kreeger Davidson's One-Image work both variety and unity depend on the ironical, unresolved relationship of the plates. Nonetheless, the coherent arrangement of the plates, that is, the sense of community evoked by their circular grouping, sets the stage—indeed, the work is a kind of stage set, an outdoor performance of abstract forms—for the later climactic, majestic *Sacella*, 1999. *Sacella* is a kind of belvedere or temple whose gestalt columns are crowned by eccentrically organic capitals. Unity seems more natural, unforced, and conspicuous here, as does variety, revealed as the toleration and proliferation of differences. Indeed, *Sacella* reconciles unity and variety; it shows the variety that is possible within unity and the unity that can emerge from and sustain variety, thus suggesting the reconciliation of opposites that makes for classical harmony. Can we interpret this life-affirming work as a

3. Ibid., p. 56

12

sacred grove of enchanted females, at last linked together in a dance of life, a stable if Dionysian relationship, in which their conflicts and differences are resolved? It had to have been difficult to achieve the dynamic tranquility—the durable resolution and noble proportions—of *Sacella*. Indeed, it took a lifetime of emotional as well as artistic work.

Kreeger Davidson's art has been split between pure geometrical form and explicit figuration from her graduate-school days. One meditative head, resembling that of the Buddha, points to her humanist and mystical side, whereas an intricate geometrical construction, with a certain resemblance to Naum Gabo's work, shows her strong, already sophisticated awareness of pure abstraction. Geometrical abstraction seems to dominate in such constructions as *Sacrifice* and *Ceremony*, both 1974, with their eccentric integration of neoprene, aluminum, and urethane—another synthetic material—but the columnar forms are implicitly totemic figures. This seems particularly clear in the dramatic *Ceremony*, a major environmental installation. The columnar forms range in height from eight to ten feet. Some are built in sections of different sizes; others are sliced open so that their inner curve is revealed. Convexity and concavity eccentrically alternate, conveying a sense of female presence. Difference is emphasized to the extent that it becomes conflict. Nonetheless, the figures are harmoniously and ritualistically arranged in a circle. They perform the ceremony together, however physically distinct they may be. Their relationship is as much a formal and constructed event as they themselves are. The struggle of Kreeger Davidson's art has been to make the formal informal: to humanize and naturalize what seems inhuman and unnatural.

Between 1979 and 1982 Kreeger Davidson made a number of Paper Puppets, such as *Black and Blue*, 1980. These figures were no doubt inspired by Indonesian puppets, but they are much more abstract and bizarre. They are at once Cubist and Surrealist—fragmented fantasy figures, on the verge of complete disintegration. Kreeger Davidson has "informalized" her figurelike columns by making them explicitly figurative, flexible, and mysterious. The puppet is a plaything, but a puppet play is about a real-life drama, often a tragic drama made comic by its representation as children's play. Kreeger Davidson's puppets, like those of Indonesia, are clearly not for children, as their hallucinatory, haunting character indicates. The puppet drawings, with their aura of menace and threat of chaos and their ghostly X-ray appearance, makes this clear. They signal yet another important breakthrough in her development, a breakthrough in which nothing is lost, but only transformed and deepened. *Isis*, *Sister*, and *Guardians*, however different their mediums, show that Kreeger Davison has not lost her geometrical dexterity, indeed, virtuosity (the geometry of these works is more intricate than it has ever previously been in her work) nor the formalist-Minimalist basis of her art. These abstract images convey a sense of movement and action that seems related to that of the puppets. The goddess and sisterhood are now on the move, socially and personally. They are forcefully alive not just formally present.

Purdah, Eloise and Abelard, Soldier, My E.T., Priestess, Circle, and *Sabah*, all made between 1985 and 1988, are tours de force of painted sculpture: a no-no according to Clement Greenberg's rules of Modernism, which demand that each medium be kept separate and pure. Lawrence Alloway notes that Kreeger Davidson's 1977 reliefs "borrow materials from painting to get some of the effects of sculpture"[4]— a play on the pictorial/sculptural mode—but in these works painting and sculpture fuse. The figure is sensualized by the vivid paint, and the paint is given body— becomes space—by the figure. These works are also particularly worthy because they make their femaleness explicit. The erotically pink petal-like curves that peel back from the stem of *Sabah*, 1986, are all but explicitly those of the labia. The other figures have openings that are vaginal in import. At the same time, the interplay of the curves seems related to that of the puppets, if more abstract. Kreeger Davidson's female has declared herself openly. She is a phallic woman in spirit, but also a peculiarly frail flower for all her strength. Referring to *Priestess II*, 1986, Kreeger Davidson writes: "The ancient, primitive, fear-laden sexual impulse has more energy for me that the geometric, landscape-oriented and optimistic, impersonal sculpture of our times. Using symmetry aided by color I was able to focus the energy on the condition of being human. Was I dealing with a new primitive world or just the fragility of being human?"

A new playfulness seems to enter Kreeger Davidson's art in the nineties. *Sirens Sing*, 1992, and *Helen and Paris*, 1994, indicate a new serenity and a new sense of integration. In the latter sculpture male and female seem equals and partners rather than antagonists in what looks like a harmonious relationship, indeed, a sexual merger. Even in *Troy*, 1994, there is an air of reciprocity between the forms, conveyed also by the fact that the differences between them seem minor. The series Days of Danger, 1995, has its violent contrasts, but the forms are also self-enclosed and sheltering—womblike—suggesting that the totemic figures, however threatening, are inwardly peaceful, that is, at one with themselves. In *Designated Angels*, 1996, the female totem acquires wings. She is ready to ascend to heaven, to escape from the earth to a more benign place. Kreeger Davidson has moved from an aggressive, austere geometrical feminist formalism to a relaxed, even joyous organic geometry and feminist formalism, perhaps most evident in *Sacella*. It is a long odyssey, one of self-discovery and self-transformation as well as artistic courage.

4. Lawrence Alloway, "Art," *The Nation*, April 16, 1977, p. 476.

CAROL KREEGER DAVIDSON'S DAYS OF DANGER

DONALD KUSPIT

The works that constitute Carol Kreeger Davidson's Days of Danger series are her most consummate rendering of the abstract figure: her most forbidding and enigmatic figures. They are at once pure constructions and archetypal personages: an uncanny synthesis of contradictory intentions.

There is a revolt against masculinist and Modernist expectations in the character of these figures: they are closed rather than open structures. They huddle in on themselves, rather than expand into the surrounding environment, and they give us presence: monumental figures, with a kind of baroque flair and fullness, that firmly stand their ground and inhabit their space. The cunning of many of Kreeger Davidson's figures is that they are not solid at the core, but they are so tightly wrapped up in themselves—almost hermetically self-enclosed—that they convey a compact presence, made more haunting by the glimpse into their inner space.

Boundaries are important for Kreeger Davidson: not only between the inner and outer and between the sculptural presence and its surroundings, but between the rigidly vertical and flexibly horizontal. Virtually all her sculptures involve an upright, totemlike element, made of aluminum rolls, which is partially encompassed by an eccentrically flexed plane of aluminum, functioning like a kind of arch or cloak. Kreeger Davidson's figures are like coiled springs: they convey a sense of pent-up—impacted—energy, waiting to explode, but under control. This is not inappropriate: they are reincarnations—abstract allegories—of Assyrian gods, and quite powerful and violent, as indicated by their attributes—all found objects that project energy. Does this assembly of mysterious figures form a new kind of Ishtar Gate? They do seem to have the same guardian function as the dangerous sacred animals on that Neo-Babylonian monument.

The shockingly real objects that are in principle the most essential part of Kreeger Davidson's abstract figures make them even more self-contradictory: The objects give the figures narrative import as well as ironical, even absurd and perverse, visual appearance. Thus, the hands of *Ninurta-Dinitu* are tied as it were—just wait until they are free and s/he attacks her/his enemies with them. *Elam* tightly hugs the sword to her/his body, having only to stretch her/his arm to thrust it into us. The machete, the axe, and the heavy rope are all clear signs of the dangerous character of Kreeger Davidson's ominous figures. The coiled rope of *Aramaic* seems to me a particularly sinister—subtly vicious—instrument of revenge, for it suggests that the goddess is ready to crush her victims in a tight embrace. The rope also makes the double meaning of Kreeger Davidson's real weapons quite clear: they are simultaneously formal devices that go against the grain of her abstract figures, giving them an unexpected expressive edge, and a means of making them important and conspicuous in the lifeworld. The figures have to be taken seriously because of their weapons. Kreeger Davidson's sculptures are thus exceptionally aggressive sociopolitical as well as unusual aesthetic statements. The provocative weapon, isolated in the abstract field of the figure, is also a sign of its estrangement and isolation. Indeed, each of Kreeger Davidson's figures stands quite alone—whatever traits it shares with the others that make it part of the same family—and seems altogether alien, not only because it is nonhuman but also because it is strange in—and to—itself.

The contrast between inner and outer surfaces is a constant feature of Kreeger Davidson's sculptures. The difference—opposition—between inner and outer surfaces reflects the difference between woman's appearance in the world and her inner reality. Inner space and outer space are not compatible—woman's body, by which the world thinks it knows her, and her inner life, by which she knows herself, are at odds. She cannot reconcile the two, and the world is as indifferent to her inner being as it is fascinated by her seductive outer appearance. It only takes notice of her inner life when she confronts it with a weapon—an unnerving manifestation of willpower. Indeed, Kreeger Davidson's figures are confrontational and peculiarly willful, however much they maintain their isolation and insularity. —1997

CIRCLE AND SPANISH BRONZES

CYNTHIA NADELMAN

Carol Kreeger Davidson's new sculptures set a standard for a particular kind of sculpture today just as surely as they occupy space. Looking at the most recent work especially, her sheet-bronze fabrications that are as much at home outdoors in Madrid as in New York, one forgets about the occasionally finicky and parochial concerns of the current sculptural scene. One forgets that there is ever a question of whether sculpture can speak to both initiates and a broader public. Davidson renders such questions moot. While she may confront a host of problems on the road to completing individual works, the problems do not take over. They do not usurp the sculpture's content.

The current sculptures are two sides of the same coin: bronze constructions fabricated at the Fabrica Magisa foundry in Madrid, where Davidson spent the spring of 1988 supervising and working without speaking the language, and the canvas-and-fiberglass-paper constructions that are these bronze works' progenitors. Both sets of sculptures are painted. The metal works, called Spanish Bronzes are variants of the earlier models, rather than copies. In spirit, they are almost an entirely new series.

Davidson's mode of operation is to fold, bend, overlap, and attach flat materials that have been cut into patterns. Issues of additive and subtractive sculpture are sidestepped in her work. It is at once both and neither. In its attitude of self-imposed rigor and consistency, this method ties in with a strain in twentieth-century sculpture that encompasses work from Russian Constructivism through Postminimalism and process art—all areas in which Davidson has a deep interest. The paper-and-canvas works' de-emphasis of luxury materials embodies this womanlike attitude. Another object of her admiration is the work of the Spanish sculptor Julio González, whose fine workmanship in constructed metal is a fitting precedent for Davidson's own Spanish project of creating a series in bronze.

Davidson's sculptures slice into space, while allowing space to circulate freely. Insides are turned out, sections are bisected or punctured, and overlaps are joined and bolted. The use of color accentuates these complexities and interrelationships, especially when—as in some of the new sculptures—the color is applied in stripes as wide and obvious as those on a barbershop pole.

The ancestral paper-and-canvas sculptures, which exist as an entity the artist calls the Circle series, seem to deliberately avoid notions of grandeur in their concern with invention and flexibility. The passage from this state to bronze keeps the metal works, in turn, from grandstanding, from giving the impression that they came into existence entirely on their own. They are still tied to their genesis in ruder, if also more ephemeral, materials. Certainly, in emulating the actions of paper and canvas, rather than clay or plaster, bronze has found itself in a new role. And Davidson enjoys exposing her means. One is reminded of an earlier piece in which the sculptor laced together two metal edges with metal lacing and then, having a good deal of the lacing left over, made a pocket in the side of the sculpture in which to put it. At once blunt and fanciful, this solution was marvelously characteristic.

With the bronze works, though, Davidson has arrived at a new level of achievement. They are seductive, like it or not, drawing the viewer into their presence. The physical properties of metal are expressively revealed. The warm shine of the exposed bronze actually makes the places of bending and coming together seem natural and organic. There are, after all, good reasons why sculptors have long worked with this material.

Although Davidson employs elements of tailoring, her sculptures never quite become figurative. In posture and stance, they may suggest the human form, or at least a human way of existing in space, but one of their sources of fascination is how they hover at this point without leaving the realm of abstract sculpture. Their size, just under human height, makes them ideal as public sculptures; they are noble and intriguing, yet approachable.

A sculpture such as *Nara* (named after the Japanese temple city), with its simple black folds, tipped cylindrical form at the top, and pinkish bronze interior, might prompt one to think of a Zen or Shinto priest, but the stance and notion of vestments make it more a priest of any religion, or rather an embodiment of priestliness, of dignity, devotion, or patience. Next to this, the spirited *Jude*, with its black and bright-bronze stripes, its sharp flying buttress of an extension, and its active three-footed base, creates a distinct contrast.

While the Circle series forms an interactive community of sculptures, the Spanish Bronzes venture into the world, each one loosening its bonds with the group. The entire body of work constitutes a bright new offering in the realm of international sculpture. — 1988

CAROL KREEGER DAVIDSON

A RETROSPECTIVE

ESSAYS BY SALLY FISHER

Above:
Reclining Figure. 1963
Newsprint, pencil
25 x 31 inches

Below:
Self-Portrait. 1964
D'Arches paper, ink, watercolor
22 x 18 inches

EARLY WORK

Queen. 1964
Bronze
15 x 5 x 4 inches

RFK. 1968
Collage
18 x 12 inches
Collection of Arnold and
Beverly Greenberg, Hartford,
Connecticut

Farther East. 1969
Bronze
30 x 18 x 24 inches
Collection of Drs. Barbara and
Stanley Edelstein, Hartford,
Connecticut

Joseph's Dream. 1963
Bronze
15 x 12 x 4 inches

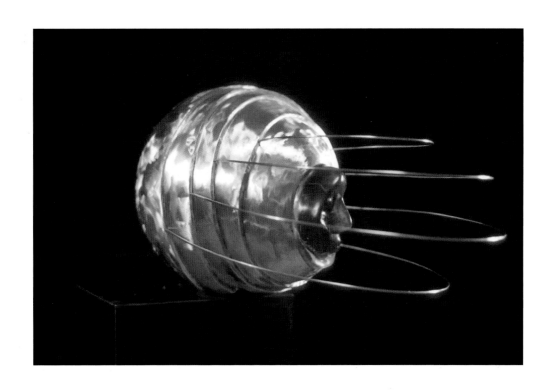

Above:
In the Beginning. 1971
1 foot 4 inches x 4 feet x 2 feet
Bronze, acrylic

Below:
In the Beginning. (detail)

Above:
Pharaoh's Children. 1967
Bronze
24 x 8 x 8 inches

Below:
Buddha. 1974
Bronze
8 x 4 x 5 inches

Shrine (three views). 1971
Wood, Formica, Kydex
6 x 5 x 4 feet

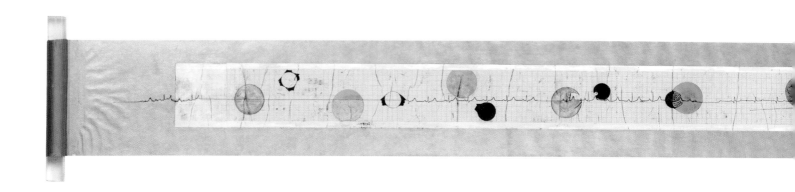

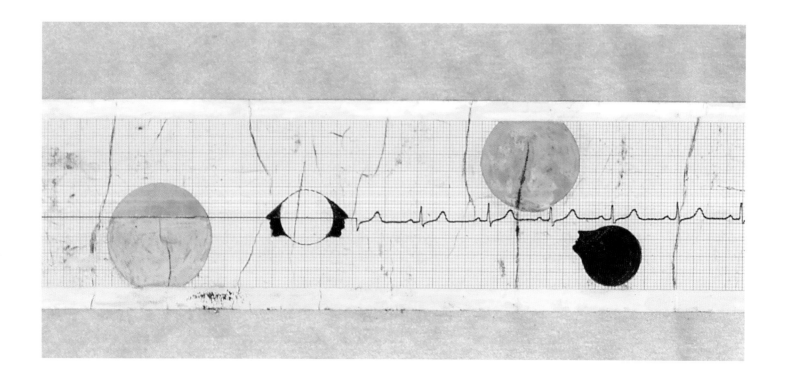

Above:
My First EKG. 1971
Acrylic and ink on paper
6 x 62 inches

Below:
My First EKG. (detail)

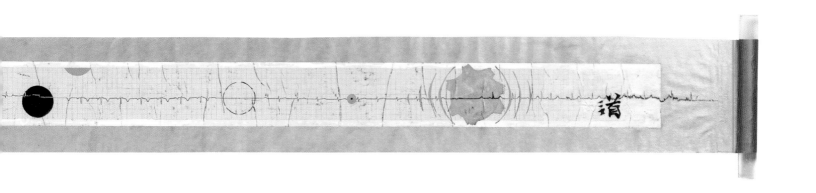

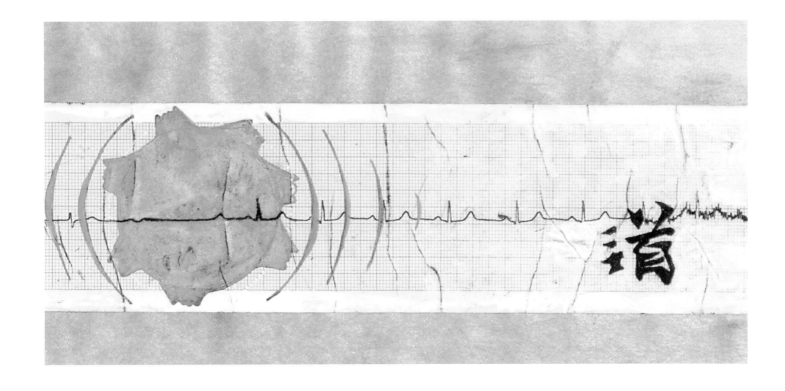

During the gasoline crisis of 1973 Kreeger Davidson was commuting to graduate school. While waiting in line at a gas station she noticed a large heap of old, discarded inner tubes. She inquired about them and was told she could take them away—as many as she wanted. Favoring the tubes that had labels, spigots, and patches, she filled her car to capacity.

For a month Kreeger Davidson did almost nothing else but sew sections of the inner tubes together, using a carpet needle and thread. Sewing can be a wry kind of feminist statement—Emily Dickinson's fascicles have been seen in this light—and this possibility was not lost on Kreeger Davidson. "I was involved in community work then," she has said, "and I made my large box (*The Big Box, The Bride and Her Husbands, Even*), piece by piece, at the meetings. I was putting everyone on to some extent, but I was transforming myself at the same time. Perhaps the spirit of my immigrant Bohemian grandmother had something to do with it; she had used her only salable skill to become, eventually, the head seamstress at Marshall Field's in Chicago. But the main thing is, you must love your material. I loved to feel neoprene, loved the way it draped, loved to sew it." *

Persephone was the last of the works in this group. "Black rubber: what could be more underworld?" the artist has said. "The title came to me immediately as I began to work, as titles almost always do. I hate to 'think up' at title. I love myths, legends, and metaphors, and that's where most of my titles come from." The title might also reflect the bifurcated nature of the sculpture—evoking Persephone's fate always to divide herself, dwelling both in life and in death.—SF

* For a more complete discussion of the feminist implications of Kreeger Davidson's neoprene work, see Donald Kuspit, "From Postminimalism to Totemism: Carol Kreeger Davidson's Journey to the Self," page 8.

The Big Box, The Bride and Her Husbands, Even (two views and detail). 1974
Neoprene inner tubes
6 x 6 x 3 feet

NEOPRENE

Above:
Ceremony. 1974
Neoprene, urethane, aluminum
11-foot circle; each piece 9
inches in diameter

Below:
Sacrifice. 1974
Neoprene, aluminum, steel
89 x 68 x 12 inches

Persephone. 1975
Neoprene, aluminum
8 feet 6 inches x 4 feet x 16 inches

In 1969 Kreeger Davidson returned with her family from a tour of duty in Borneo with the Peace Corps. On the trip back she spent a week in Cambodia, exploring the interior of Angkor Wat. The temple complex's dancing apasaras and stone pillars encased in stone frames utterly captivated her imagination. She made countless drawings of the magical pillars, and her sketchbook remained the constant reference as she created the Paper Pillars.

Before designing an installation, the artist would examine a site's walls for quirks, turns, plumbing fixtures, corners, and would then make a rough diagram with dimensions. Corners were especially interesting, as was anything that created an obstacle. The Paper Pillars transform static space into a dynamic sequence much like a narrative frieze but without the story. Their allusion to ancient architecture is almost masked by their cleansed simplicity of form.

Use of neoprene cord came naturally out of Kreeger Davidson's earlier experience with neoprene. She structured the works by making lines with pushpins and cord, stretching and sometimes weaving the cord, and then inserting the paper. Thanks to the help of her niece, an interior designer, she discovered a supplier of a large and heavy fiberglass paper with a deckle edge. The paper took paint beautifully and had considerable strength. She bought 3,000 sheets and for a while worked with almost no other material. –S F

Photograph taken by the artist at the temple complex, Angkor Wat, Cambodia, 1969.

PAPER PILLARS

Paper Pillars I. 1975
Installation, Soho Center
of Visual Arts, New York
Arches Cover paper,
neoprene cord, pushpins
4 feet x 26 feet x 8 inches

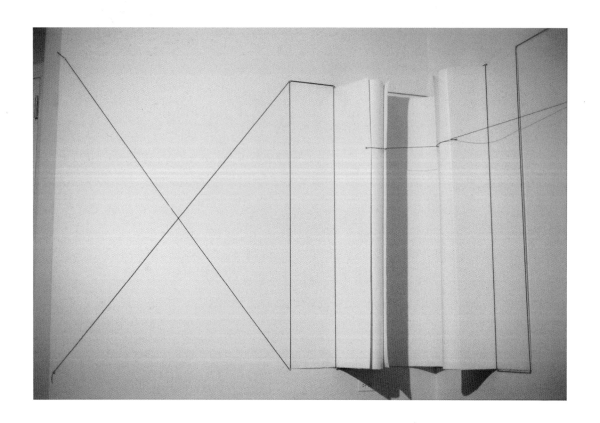

Above:
Paper Pillars IV. 1978
Installation, home of
Suzanne and Bucky Weil,
Minneapolis, Minnesota
Arches Cover paper, neoprene
cord, pushpins
48 feet x 17 feet x 8 inches

Below:
Last Chapter ("Caught in Time,"
number 8). 1978
Installation, Gloria Cortella
Gallery, New York
Fiberglass paper, neoprene
cord, pushpins
5 feet 8 ½ inches x 12 feet x
12 inches

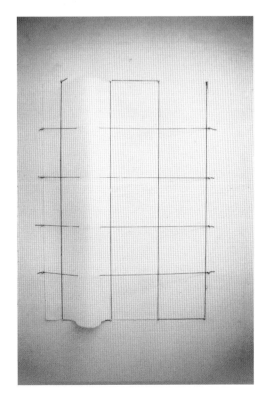

Above:
Paper Pillars II. 1977
Installation, Trinity College,
Hartford, Connecticut
Fiberglass paper, acrylic,
neoprene cord, pushpins
5 feet 8 inches x 28 feet x
8 inches

Below:
3-Row Paper Pillar. 1979
Arches Cover paper,
neoprene cord, pushpins
48 x 36 x 6 inches

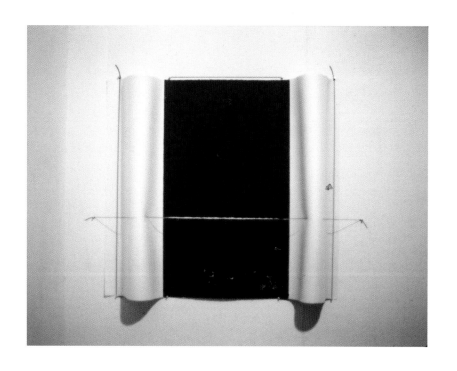

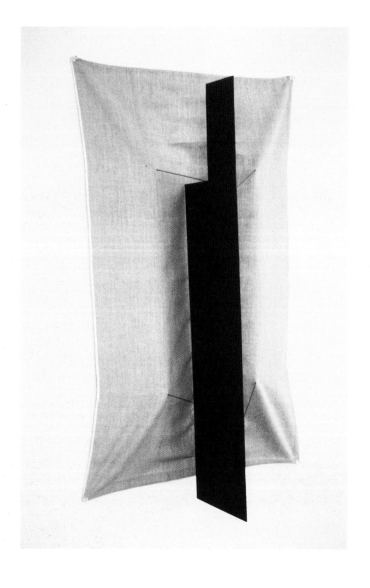

Above:
Dürga. 1977
Arches Cover paper,
neoprene cord, pushpins
42 x 43 x 7 ½ inches

Below:
Koan II. 1978
Linen, wood, neoprene cord
36 x 24 x 14 inches
Collection of Mr. and Mrs.
Carlos Dyer, Ridgefield,
Connecticut

Facing page, above:
Burden of Content II. 1978
Installation, Museum of
Modern Art, New York
Arches Cover paper,
neoprene cord, pushpins
4 feet x 14 feet x 10 inches

Below:
Paper Pillars III. 1977
Installation, Invitational
Exhibition, John Weber Gallery,
New York
Fiberglass paper, neoprene
cord, pushpins
5 feet x 28 feet x 8 inches

Isis. 1975
One-quarter inch aluminum
plates and nails, neoprene cord
74 x 90 x 14 inches
Aldrich Museum of
Contemporary Art, Ridgefield,
Connecticut

Facing page:
Isis Split Up. 1975
Aluminum, neoprene cord
65 x 58 x 11 inches
Collection of Dr. and Mrs.
Charles Gibbs, Santa Fe,
New Mexico

ISIS, DANCE OF LIFE, CANVAS PILLARS

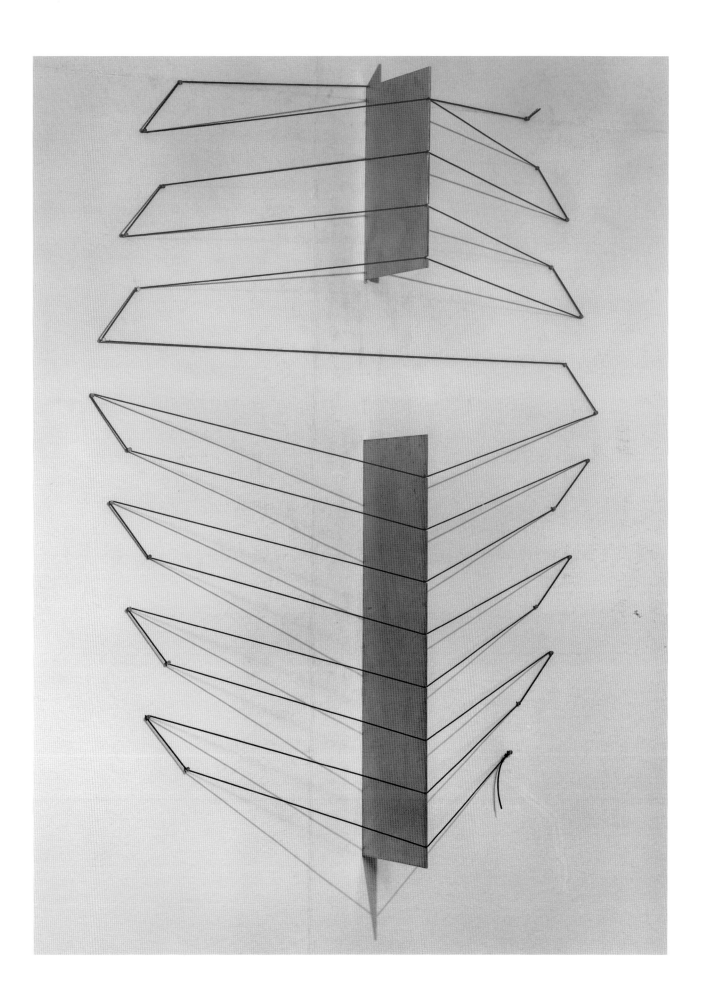

41

Dance of Life (two views). 1975
Aluminum, neoprene cord
10-foot circle; each piece
6 feet x 24 inches
New Jersey State Museum,
Trenton, gift of Dr. and Mrs.
Charles Gibbs, 1982

Above:
Gate. 1977
Canvas, aluminum, acrylic
72 x 80 x 9 inches

Below:
Thin Red Line. 1977
Canvas, aluminum,
neoprene cord
6 feet 11 inches x
9 feet 1 inch x 12 inches
Collection of Mr. and Mrs.
Mark Hellinger, Greenwich,
Connecticut

Wall Guardians. 1979
Fiberglass paper, neoprene cord,
fiberglass tape, acrylic
7 feet 7 inches x 19 feet 9 inches
x 8 inches

Facing page:
Guardians. 1979
Fiberglass paper, neoprene cord,
fiberglass tape, acrylic
90 $^1/_2$ x 39 $^3/_4$ inches

INVITATIONAL EXHIBITION: ROSE ART MUSEUM, BRANDEIS UNIVERSITY

Guardians and *Wall Guardians*

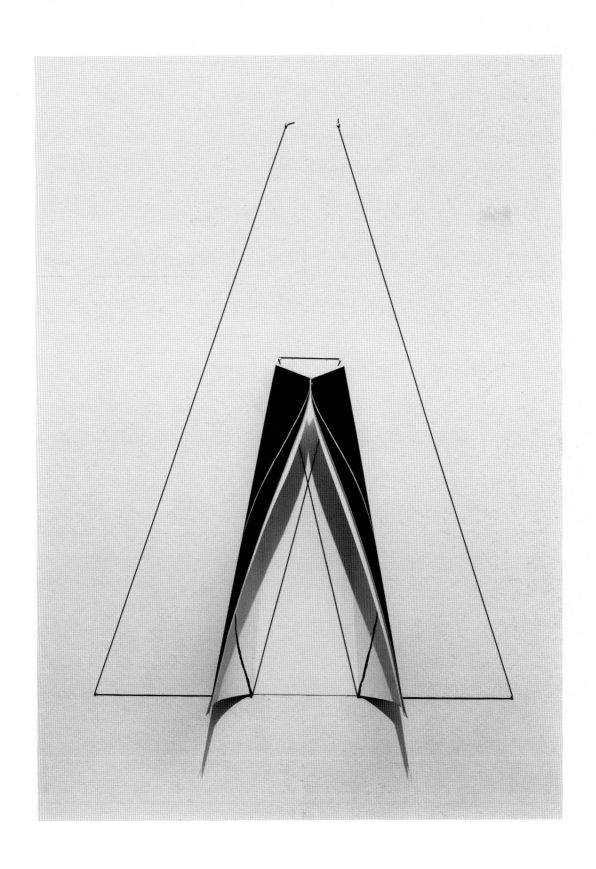

Sister. 1979
Fiberglass paper, neoprene cord,
fiberglass tape, acrylic
83 x 62 x 20 inches

Above:
Ziggurat. 1978
Velour paper, litho crayon
20 x 26 inches

Below:
Square Spaces. 1973
Graph paper, litho crayon
30 x 24 inches

Facing page:
My Eye. 1974
Stonehenge paper, film, ink
24 x 19 ¹/₄ inches

DRAWINGS

the eye.
BY WHICH I
see god is the
same as the eye B
y which god sees me.
My eye AND god's eye a
re one AND the same
one in seeing
one in knowing
An One in

Above:
Study for Architectural Sculpture II. 1972
Arches Cover paper, litho crayon
29 x 41 inches

Below:
Study for Architectural Sculpture I. 1972
Arches Cover paper, litho crayon
41 x 29 inches

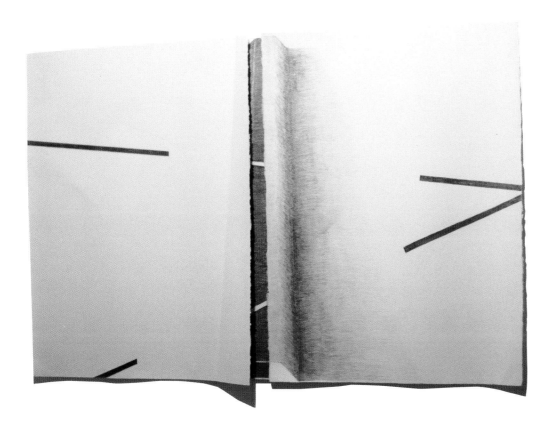

Above:
Paper Pillar Drawing. 1978
Arches Cover paper (buff),
pencil
24 x 30 inches
Collection of Dr. and Mrs.
Melvin Goldstein, Hartford,
Connecticut

Below:
Paper Pillar Drawing with Tape.
1979
Arches Cover paper, pencil,
paper tape
30 x 42 inches

Voluptuous in spite of their materials—sheets of paper laminated to linen and joined by bolts—the Paper Puppets evoke an enormous range of contradictory emotions. A puppet is a creature controlled by another, yet, even without their titles, *Black and Blue* and *Hanging On* suggest an even more ominous plight than that of being controlled. Though on one level they may reflect the darker side of a man's wish for a paper doll "to call his own," they go beyond gender struggles almost to theological ones. Suspended in implacable, inescapable stasis, these puppets have been abandoned by the puppeteer.

The buoyant leap of *Thank You, Matisse* is another matter. The Paper Puppet series marked Kreeger Davidson's return to the figure, an irresistible move but one about which she had felt many doubts. An encounter with Matisse's *Pink Nude* convinced the artist that no choice between abstraction and the figure was really necessary. The place between the two would become most fruitful for her. *Thank You, Matisse* celebrates the joy in that liberating discovery.

Self Lovers takes on isolation and loneliness with quietly defiant pleasure, and the two-sided *Crossing the Styx* plunges us into the ancient and terrifying world of mythic imagination. *Markdowns,* a much later work, recalls the Paper Puppets but introduces a powerful social comment. These hanging silhouettes make a witty yet painfully direct reference to those members of humanity passed over and devalued.–S F

Paper Puppets in the artist's studio.

Facing page:
Hanging On. 1981
Fiberglass paper, canvas, acrylic
72 x 48 inches
Collection of Susanne and Larry
Spencer, Louisville, Kentucky

PAPER PUPPETS AND PUPPET DRAWINGS

Black and Blue. 1980
Fiberglass paper, canvas, acrylic
78 x 34 x 22 inches

Facing page:
Black and Blue (detail)

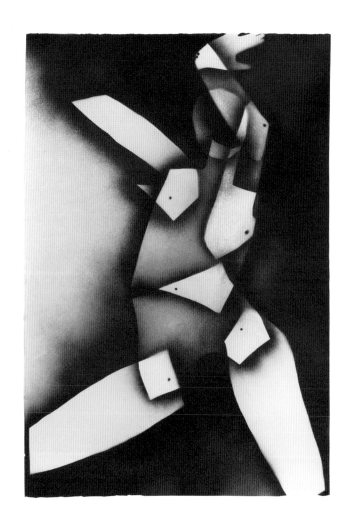

Above left:
Puppet Drawing IV. 1979
Arches Cover paper, acrylic, ink
48 x 29 ¹/₂ inches
Collection of Brian MacDonald,
Towanda, Pennsylvania

Right:
Puppet Drawing V. 1979
Arches Cover paper, acrylic, pencil
48 x 31 ¹/₂ inches

Facing page, above:
Puppet Drawing VIII. 1980
Arches Cover paper, acrylic
48 x 31 inches
Collection of Mary and Leigh
Block Museum of Art,
Northwestern University,
Evanston, Illinois

Below:
Self Lovers. 1979
Arches Cover paper, acrylic
48 inches x 9 feet 2 inches

Crossing the Styx (light side). 1980
Canvas, fiberglass paper, acrylic
10 feet x 12 feet x 10 inches

Facing page:
Crossing the Styx (dark side)

Thank You, Matisse. 1982
Fiberglass paper, canvas, acrylic
40 x 32 x 15 inches
Collection of Joanne and
James Alter, Chicago

Markdowns. 1994
Cardboard, acrylic, steel rack
78 x 30 x 58 inches

The abstract figure answered Kreeger Davidson's need to speak to the human condition. The figure by definition carries this content, but its abstract treatment gave the artist freedom to invent and thus to tap new sources of emotional and metaphoric expression.

The artist enjoyed working with malleable and comparatively lightweight materials. But much as she loved the qualities of fiberglass paper and canvas, she was aware that, given the scale of the work she was most interested in, the next, logical step was toward metal.

Kreeger Davidson started with an aluminum version of the fiberglass *Priestess*. The change of medium was a complex one; it took her three months to complete the sculpture. Then, moving to sheet bronze, she made *Eloise and Abelard* in six days.—S F

Purdah. 1985
Fiberglass paper, canvas, acrylic
84 x 14 1/2 x 44 inches

ABSTRACT FIGURES 1985-86

Priestess. 1986
Canvas, fiberglass paper, acrylic,
neoprene cord
75 x 27 ¹/₂ x 24 inches

Priestess II. 1986
Aluminum, acrylic
84 x 26 ¹/₂ x 24 inches
Collection of Dr. Makoto
Hozumi, Akita, Japan

Kadazan. 1986
Patinated bronze
28 x 12 $\frac{1}{2}$ x 14 $\frac{1}{2}$ inches

Facing page:
Sabah. 1986
Canvas, fiberglass paper, acrylic
72 x 29 x 14 inches

Facing page and above:
Eloise and Abelard
(two indoor views). 1986
Bronze, acrylic
25 x 18 ³/₄ x 54 inches
58 x 21 ¹/₂ x 31 ¹/₂ inches

Below:
Eloise and Abelard
(in the subway, New York).

Kreeger Davidson wanted to create a "family" of sculptures or, more accurately, a group that for her would represent the whole of the human environment. *Circle* came out of this impulse. She chose the names for the individual sculptures in the group from various languages, often using alphabets sent at her request from some of New York City's foreign embassies.

In the meantime, a selection of her sculptures, including *Eloise and Abelard,* was shown at the annual ARCO (Fiera Internacional de Arte Contempraneo) exhibition in Madrid in 1988. Representatives of the Magisa foundry and art gallery saw the work and asked the artist's dealer, Richard Humphrey, whether the artist who had done the sculpture might want "his" work fabricated at their foundry; they could offer a good price, because they expected in turn to learn something from "him." Without correcting their pronouns, Humphrey replied that the artist had seven sculptures ready to fabricate in bronze.*

Kreeger Davidson immediately made paper models of the fiberglass-paper-and-linen forms from *Circle* and went to Spain. While the men at the foundry recovered from their shock at the artist's gender, Kreeger Davidson found a female translator, whom she needed for both communication and morale. Two men from the foundry and the two women worked, together with the many other foundry workers, for seven weeks, completing all of the Spanish Bronzes except *Erik the Red*, which the artist created just after returning to Hartford, Connecticut. While making adjustments on the piece, she took it apart, intending to join the two parts again. But once she saw the work in two sections, she preferred it that way. A continuing interest in two-part sculptures has been the result of that discovery. —SF

* For an extended critical essay, "Circle and Spanish Bronzes," by Cynthia Nadelman, see page 17.

CIRCLE, SPANISH BRONZES, ERIK THE RED

Circle. 1988
Fiberglass paper, linen
Each unit 4 feet

Circle (another view)
Fiberglass paper, linen

Models for Spanish Bronzes. 1988
Fiberglass paper

Above:
Russ. 1988
Bronze, acrylic
61 ³/₄ x 21 ¹/₄ x 47 ³/₄ inches

Below:
De Rapiña. 1988
Bronze, acrylic
65 x 23 x 41 inches
Collection of Sol and Carol LeWitt

Above:
Jefe. 1988
Bronze, acrylic
62 $\frac{1}{2}$ x 36 x 38 inches

Below:
Jude. 1988
Bronze, acrylic
60 x 42 $\frac{3}{4}$ x 40 inches

Above:
Nara. 1988
Bronze, acrylic
63 x 60 x 58 inches
Collection of the National
Museum of Women in the Arts,
Washington, D.C.

Below:
Genji. 1989
Bronze
Left: 66 x 31 x 28 inches
Right: 60 x 30 x 19 inches
Collection of Mr. and Mrs.
Allen Coleman, Highland Park,
Illinois

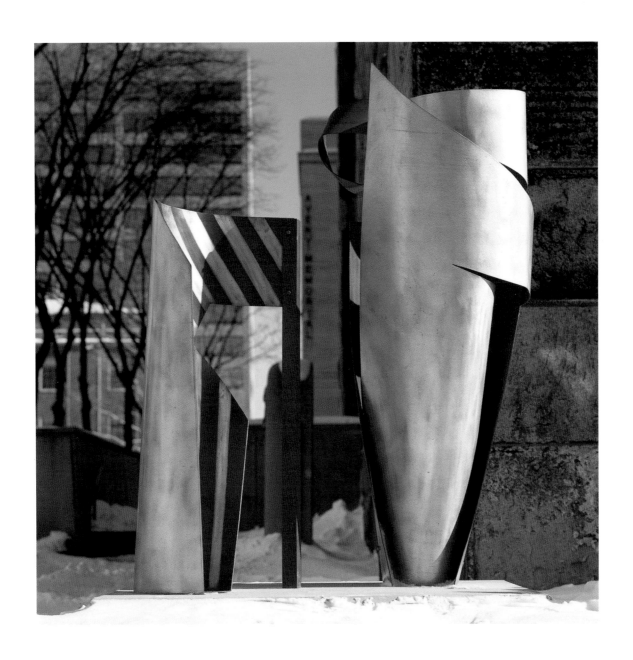

Erik the Red (sited in front of the Wadsworth Atheneum Museum of Art, two views). 1989
Bronze, acrylic
48 x 22 x 18 inches
65 x 73 x 20 inches
Collection of the Wadsworth Atheneum Museum of Art, Hartford, Connecticut

ABSTRACT FIGURES 1990—91

First Settler. 1990
Canvas, fiberglass paper, acrylic
34 x 21 x 16 inches

Sheba (Queen of). 1990
Bronze, aluminum, acrylic
60 x 48 x 33 inches
Collection of the Eaton
Corporation, Cleveland, Ohio

Ruth and Naomi. 1990
Fiberglass paper, linen, acrylic
Each figure: 69 x 56 x 17 inches

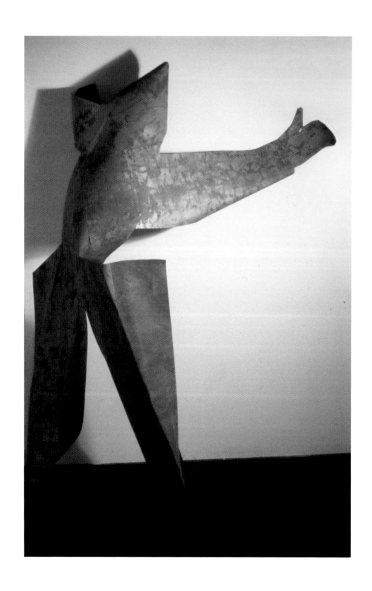

Above:
Head-line. 1992
Bronze, acrylic
43 x 43 x 21 inches

Below:
Samson. 1990
Fiberglass paper, linen, acrylic
76 x 66 ¹/₂ x 26 ¹/₂ inches
Collection of the Eaton
Corporation, Cleveland, Ohio

Potiphar's Wife. 1990
Bronze, steel, acrylic
Left: 50 x 15 inches
Right: 46 x 27 x 52 inches
Collection of Richard Humphrey,
New York

Indra. 1990
Bronze, stainless steel
87 x 18 x 23 inches

Facing page:
David Goliath. 1991
Bronze, acrylic
78 x 88 x 33 inches
Collection of Lyman Allyn Art
Museum, Connecticut College,
New London

J. C. 1992
Fiberglass paper, flocked
wallpaper, acrylic, plywood
84 x 48 x 29 inches

FIBERGLASS FIGURES ON WALLPAPERED PLYWOOD

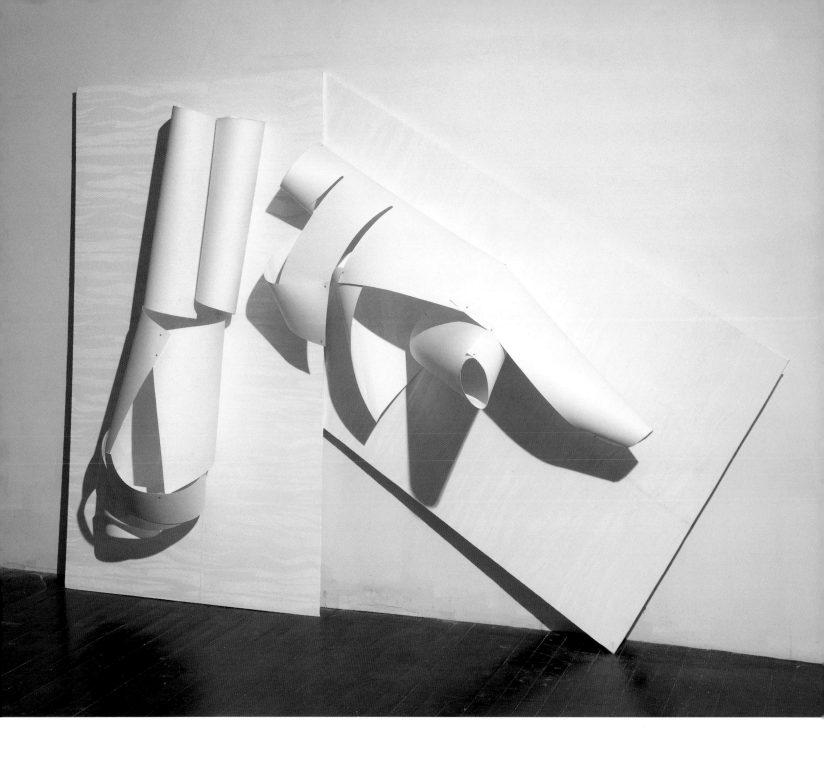

Upside Down and Sideways. 1992
Fiberglass paper, flocked
wallpaper, plywood, acrylic
84 x 96 x 31 inches

Facing page:
Euro-Apsaras (two views). 1992
Fiberglass paper, wallpaper,
acrylic, plywood
Group: 84 inches x 28 feet x
30 inches

The Sirens who sang to Jason and Odysseus made their gorgeous music for only one purpose, to lure and destroy the enchanted seafarers. Kreeger Davidson's Sirens are far less sinister. For one thing, they have for the first time made themselves visible, a fact full of feminist implications. And, surprisingly, they seem to sing joyously, for themselves, for one another. The reach of their "arms" is out and then back again, echoing the movement of the curling waves. Perhaps they simply love to sing.

In creating this work, the artist moved again in the direction of abstraction, although her figures still embody human gesture. The stripes Kreeger Davidson likes so much to use may hark back to her early love of ancient Egyptian artifacts, but they also introduce color without obscuring the rich bronze surface; they let her have it both ways.

The bronze waves that keep these enigmatic creatures at a slight distance from us (see page 92) present a fascinating contradiction: hard water. They enact the flow and movement of the surf while at the same time implying the rocks beyond.—SF

Sirens Sing. 1992
Bronze, acrylic
Individual figures:
72 x 32 x 45 inches
Group: 6 feet x 8 feet 6
inches x 9 feet 8 inches
Collection of the Eaton
Corporation, Cleveland, Ohio

SIRENS SING

Sirens Sing (as installed at Mary
and Leigh Block Museum of
Art, Northwestern University,
Evanston, Illinois)
Waves: 12 ¹/₂ x 27 x 69 inches

Facing page:
Sirens Sing (another view)

INCA / NAZCA

Guardians. 1986
Arches Cover paper, pencil
48 x 30 inches

Inca/Nazca (two views). 1993
Aluminum, Tuffak
Each section: 91 ¹/₂ x 48 x
39 ¹/₂ inches

DRAWINGS ON WALLPAPER

Above left:
Bowing. 1993
Wallpaper, acrylic
44 x 30 inches

Right:
Blackswirl. 1992
Wallpaper, acrylic
44 x 30 inches

Above:
Black Double Head. 1992
Wallpaper, acrylic
44 x 30 inches
Collection of Sol and Carol LeWitt

Below:
Wallpaper Drawing IX. 1993
Wallpaper, acrylic
30 x 44 inches
Collection of Jerry and Elaine
Lowengard, West Hartford,
Connecticut

Starting with a large sheet of paper, as she almost always does, Kreeger Davidson bends, cuts, bends again, and, using a punch, "buttons up" her preliminary figure with stainless-steel bolts. The transition from paper to sheet metal is a logical one. "Anything you can do with paper you can do with sheet metal," she says.

Medea and the works related to *Troy* have the uncanny expressiveness that comes from their being neither wholly abstract nor wholly figurative. "My sculpture is always a struggle between the closure of figure and the opening of abstract form. It's the tension between the two—that uneasy place between geometric and organic; between the inside where the private drama unfolds and the outside skin that touches the world."

Medea, at once regal, wounded, and murderous, recalls the poisoned crown with which Medea killed her rival. The *Cassandras* seem to stare into the dark tunnel of the future, though they hardly have eyes. The *Soldiers* simultaneously attack, run in retreat, and fall, splayed in death. *Paris and Helen* seem to shrink from the larger world into their tightly bent embrace as if caught in a trance, which indeed they are, having fallen under the spell of Aphrodite. In *Troy*, the central work, a victor, a fallen figure, and a fleeing one—all three scarred—hover and fall on a tilted battleground. The sculptor identifies them as Achilles, the dead Hector, and Briseis. Briseis was first abducted from her home and then traded off between Achilles and Agamemnon in the war of pride they waged within the war between the Achaeans and the Trojans—that war also waged within a larger one, the overriding battle among the gods. From the beginning of her career, Kreeger Davidson has believed that "the tension between the story and the form holds the mystery and the resonance of art."–SF

TROY AND MEDEA

Troy. 1994
Bronze, acrylic
6 feet x 9 feet 5 inches x
48 inches

Helen and Paris. 1994
Bronze, acrylic
23 x 28 x 15 inches

Facing page:
Medea. 1994
Aluminum, acrylic,
paving stones
68 x 24 x 27 3/4 inches

Soldiers. 1994
Fiberglass paper, linen, acrylic
Installation 60 feet long

Cassandras. 1994
Fiberglass paper, linen, acrylic
75 x 14 x 16 inches

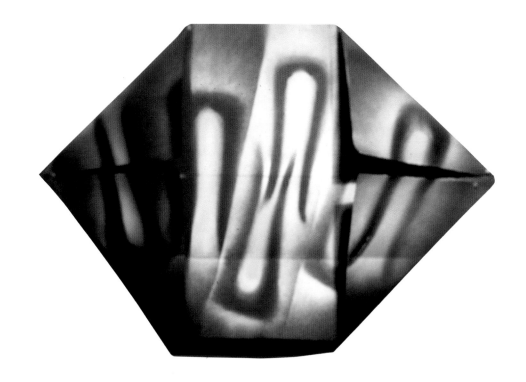

Above:
Black Fold. 1994
Arches Cover paper, acrylic
29 x 41 inches

Below:
Key Lock. 1994
Arches Cover paper, acrylic
29 x 41 inches

Facing page, above:
Five Key. 1994
Arches Cover paper, acrylic
32 x 44 inches

Below:
Key Hole. 1994
Arches Cover paper, acrylic
22 x 30 inches
Collection of Lita and Albert
Marks, Jr., West Hartford,
Connecticut

DRAWINGS 1994—2001

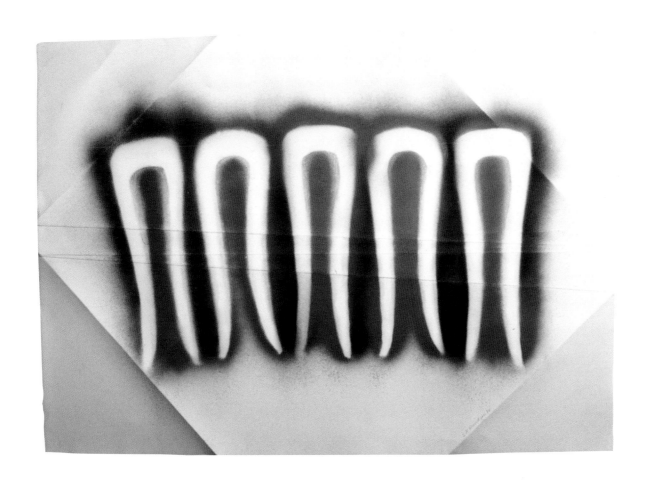

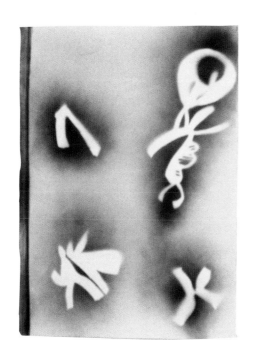

Genomes. 2000
Arches Cover paper, acrylic, pencil
Small drawings: 30 x 24 inches;
24 x 30 inches
Large drawing: 48 x 30 inches

Song II. 1989
Arches Cover paper, acrylic,
pencil, airbrush
49 x 31 ½ inches

Above left:
Quarrel. 1989
Arches Cover paper, acrylic,
pencil, airbrush
41 $^1/_2$ x 31 $^1/_2$ inches

Above right:
Balloons. 1989
Arches Cover paper, acrylic,
pencil, airbrush
41 $^1/_2$ x 31 $^1/_2$ inches

Left:
Cat's Cradle. 1990
Arches Cover paper, acrylic,
28 x 41 inches

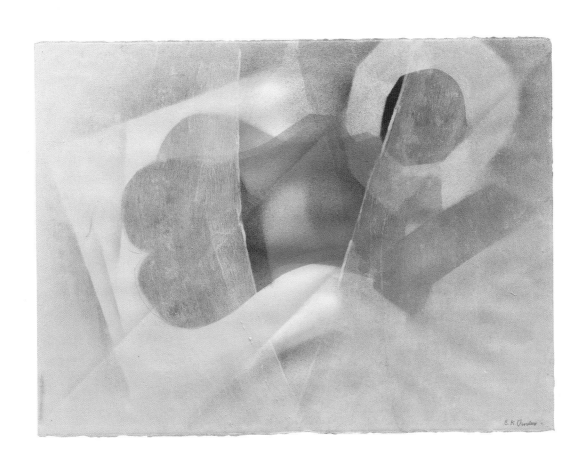

The Veil. 2001
Arches Cover paper, acrylic, gel
25 x 32 ¹/₂ inches

Kreeger Davidson's abstract figures almost always constitute an exterior surface folded around a hollow interior. When these figures appear in groups, they seem to wear a kind of benign uniform, sometimes reminiscent of religious garb. In the Days of Danger group, this exterior suddenly becomes both protective and aggressive; it appears as armor.

Late in 1994, the artist was accosted by an armed robber. Though he quickly fled, and Kreeger Davidson was not particularly shaken by the experience at the time, she found the city streets newly threatening for a while.

Several months later Kreeger Davidson began to make paper models of a group, without the intention of making its members at all ferocious. Yet, at the same time, and without any conscious purpose, she had begun to collect weapons—an Arabic sword in Jerusalem, an antique Bedouin gun at Petra, a machete in Jamaica. Such things, she has said, were "not part of my vocabulary."

Days of Danger uses the artist's customary forms with new meaning.* Their interiors suggest, for the first time, an ominous emptiness. They hover in an uneasy but absolute balance between their outer stance of fearsome aggressiveness and their inner anxiety. Far from suggesting the rather uncomplicated attempted robbery that may possibly have inspired them, the figures and their weapons evoke the full weight of human history, ancient and contemporary.—S F

* For Donald Kuspit's essay "Carol Kreeger Davidson's Days of Danger," see page 15.

DAYS OF DANGER

Days of Danger. 1995
Six of the seven elements,
left to right:

Nimrud.
Aluminum, acrylic
77 x 36 x 20 inches

Dervish.
Aluminum, acrylic
88 x 24 x 21 inches

Aramaic.
Aluminum, rope
78 x 32 x 37 inches

Ninurta-Dinitu.
Aluminum, acrylic
72 x 30 x 28 inches

Elam.
Aluminum, acrylic
77 x 36 x 20 inches

Pazuzu.
Aluminum, acrylic
63 x 50 x 12 inches

Following pages:
Ninurta-Dinitu with *Aramaic;*
Pazuzu.

DESIGNATED ANGELS

Designated Angels. 1996
Aluminum, acrylic
Large figures:
73 x 15 x 23 inches
Smaller figure:
56 x 9 x 18 inches
Smallest figure:
24 x 19 x 38 inches

Another view and details
of *Designated Angels*

In ancient Rome the *sacellum* was a small temple open to the sky; *sacello* in modern Italian. With a simple variation in spelling Kreeger Davidson has, characteristically, made her temple feminine.

Sacella followed the making of Days of Danger and came out of a long-held wish to make sculpture that would be truly and success-fully "interactive." *Inca/Nazca* (1993) reflects this wish, as does one of her earliest works, *Shrine* (1971); both are welcoming structures, meant to be entered and used, not just viewed.

Some years ago a riding accident left the artist with multiple back injuries, forcing upon her long periods when she was unable to work. The extent of her reading has proved one positive result. The ambition to create a place of rest and refreshment, a gift to friends and strangers alike, is another.

The refreshment to be found within *Sacella* is more than physical. The floral forms embellished with stained glass, inspired by the opulent mosaics at the Cathedral of Santa Maria la Nuova, Monreale, Sicily, and the "writing" perforating the arms of the sculpture—Islamic in feeling but without verbal meaning—elicit an unmistakably spiritual response. —SF

Sacella. 1999
Aluminum, stained glass
12 x 12 x 11 feet
Collection of the New Britain
Museum of American Art,
New Britain, Connecticut

SACELLA

Sacella (another view and details)

Reconstructed Issues began as a formal exercise. Craving the freedom of an entirely nonfigurative work, Kreeger Davidson started with cardboard, which, by its very stiffness, made organic form almost impossible. She created elements that could be shifted about into many configurations, a process precluded by working with the human figure, however abstract. She wanted also to use as many materials as possible, to see whether they would speak with their own voices or could harmonize and become one. She managed to employ bronze, wood, stainless steel, and aluminum—joined, as usual, with bolts. Kreeger Davidson had no myths, stories, or even a title in mind. The ironic title she eventually chose reveals a wish to move away from categories and cant.

Reconstructed Issues is made of two sections that can be moved and placed in various relationships to one another: that is, reconstructed, not deconstructed. It provides a wonderful example of the kinds of surface treatments Kreeger Davidson has employed over the years: perforations, stencils (first used on her Paper Puppets), burnishing, and painting. The piece draws the viewer around and around it, perhaps looking for the door. "Inside" and "outside" become, teasingly, its subject. While the artist insists that *Reconstructed Issues* is abstract and not a dwelling, and while it is true that the stairs are unclimbable, it is difficult not to feel led, at last, to a hearth.—SF

Reconstructed Issues. 2000
Bronze, stainless steel,
aluminum, teak
8 feet x 4 feet 6 inches x 7 feet

Following pages: alternate
views of *Reconstructed Issues*

RECONSTRUCTED ISSUES

Telamone. 2001
Bronze, pressure-treated wood,
plastic (shroud)
5 feet 6 inches x
10 feet 6 inches x 5 feet

TELAMONE

Telamone (another view, without shroud)

Facing page:
Telamone (details)

IF THEIR THOUGHTS
ARE STRONG

BORNEO PLAYBACK

CAROL KREEGER DAVIDSON

In 1967 my husband joined the Peace Corps, and we went with our two children to live in Kota Kinabalu, Sabah, Malaysia. After recovering from culture shock I fell in love with Sabah and its people. While Don was attending Peace Corps conferences and visiting volunteers at their posts, Justin Stimol invited me and the children to stay in Penampang, the largest Kadazan village in Sabah.

Justin Stimol was a musician and poet. He was passionately involved in Kadazan culture, the myths, legends, and the ancient time. The children and I listened to the elders' stories, learned to dance *sumazow* and watched a priestess perform a healing.

When I left Sabah in 1968 Justin asked me to tell the story of his people. I explained that sculptors don't tell stories. He replied, "You are one of Jack Kennedy's children. Therefore you will find a way."

Fourteen years of letters proved my friend was right. I learned video from Richard Foreman of the Ontologiacal-Hysterical Theater. There I met Babette Mangolte, Foreman's camerawoman. Two years of fund-raising, six months at New York University film school, learning, planning, with frequent disappointments followed. In 1982 Babette, Chi Chin Lui (a Chinese-American video engineer), and I flew Malaysia Airlines halfway around the world to tell the Kadazan story.

Making the video had great importance to my creative life. The film crew and I lived with Justin's family. His eldest daughter Surella was my goddaughter from Peace Corps days. I began to understand the unique Kadazan caringness: they suppressed emotion in order to protect one another from hurt. The daily routines of meals, rice cultivation, and caring for each other always included us.

The figure, always part of my work, became more important. The Kadazan sense of community made a deep impression on me; I began to make figures in a group. As I began to make larger sculpture I worked, without speaking Spanish, in a Spanish fabrica with forty workmen to complete seven sculptures. Without the Kadazan lesson I could not have managed. The complex effort of living and working together without any confrontation made it possible.

Most important of all I learned the meaning of *dau dau*. *Dau dau* refers to the natural world. Sharing Kadazan life, the film crew began to relate to nature in a more protective way. Dau dau keeps the world in balance. In those days they learned from us and we learned from them. The video was finished in 1985 in New York with Shu Lea Cheang as editor. *Borneo Playback* was the first film ever to be made about Sabah. It aired on the Public Broadcasting System in June 1985.

CHRONOLOGY

Born Carol Kreeger, Chicago, Illinois.

1935-41
Attends University of Chicago Laboratory School.

1943-44
Attends the Four-Year College at the University of Chicago.

1945
Transfers to Northwestern University. Takes courses in art history

1950
Graduates from Northwestern University with a B.A. in literature.

1951
Marries Donald Davidson.
Moves to Hartford, Connecticut.

1952-53
Teaches English and art at Sedgewick Junior High School, West Hartford, Connecticut.

1954
Birth of first child, Cynthia.

1957
Birth of second child, Jeffrey.

1958
Sustains multiple back injuries in a riding accident.

1959
Decides to study art. Spends most of the year in bed recovering from the riding accident, reading Gyorgy Kepes, László Moholy-Nagy, Henri Focillon, and other modern art theorists supplied by the head of the painting department at the Hartford Art School.

1960-61
Studies sculpture privately with Wolfgang Behl, teacher of sculpture at the University of Hartford Art School.

1963
Enters the University of Hartford Art School as a full-time student.

1967
Graduates from the University of Hartford Art School, B.F.A. cum laude, with honors in sculpture.
Travels with husband and children to Sabah, Malaysia (formerly North Borneo), for a tour of duty in the Peace Corps. Husband takes charge of Peace Corps office in Kota Kinabalu; children attend Chinese school. Works on sculpture, which is cast at the foundry of the local Public Works Department. Teaches drawing at Kent College, Tauran, and sculpture at a Chinese secondary school.

1968
Lectures on art in secondary school and at Gaya College, Kota Kinabalu.

Above:
The artist with her husband, Donald Davidson,
and *Farther East*, 1969

Right:
The artist with *Shrine*, 1971

1969
Returns with family to Hartford by way
 of Cambodia and India, visiting temples
 and sketching.
Works as visiting artist in elementary school,
 Bristol, Connecticut.

1970
Begins to commute to graduate school at the
 Rhode Island School of Design.

1973
Work shown at the Museum of Art, Rhode
 Island School of Design, and in the "New
 Talent" exhibition at Terry Dintenfass Gallery,
 New York. Receives M.F.A. fellowship and
 teaches basic drawing at Rhode Island
 School of Design.

1974
The Big Box, The Bride and Her Husbands, Even
Sacrifice
Ceremony

Receives M.F.A. from Rhode Island School
 of Design.
One-woman show at the New Britain Museum
 of American Art, New Britain, Connecticut.
Rents a studio in New York City.
Included in a group show at Terry Dintenfass
 Gallery.

1975
Persephone
Paper Pillars series begun.
Isis
Isis Split
Isis Split Up
Dance of Life
One-woman show at Soho Center of Visual
 Arts, New York.
Represented by Betty Parsons until her death
 in 1976.
Studies video with Richard Foreman at
 Connecticut College. Produces *Cat's Cradle*,
 a six-minute video piece in black and white.

At the opening of Kreeger Davidson's one-woman show at the New Britain Museum of American Art, New Britain, Connecticut, 1974. Seated around *The Big Box, The Bride and Her Husbands, Even*, left to right: James Elliot, then director of the Wadsworth Atheneum; Michael Mahoney, director of the art department, Trinity College, Connecticut; Tony Keller, director of the Connecticut Commission on the Arts; the artist, Charles Ferguson, director of the New Britain Museum of American Art.

1976

Two-artist show at the Institute of
  Contemporary Art, Boston.

1977

Gate

Thin Red Line

One-woman show at the Bonino Gallery,
  New York.

One-woman show at Rose Art Museum,
  Brandeis University.

1978

One-woman shows at Gloria Cortella Gallery,
  New York, and at the Austin Arts Center,
  Trinity College, Hartford, Connecticut.

Son Jeffrey becomes seriously ill.

Begins work on Paper Puppets.

1979

Wall Guardians

Guardians

Sister

One-woman show at the Neill Gallery,
  New York.

Makes *Family Games*, a 19-minute video
  piece in color.

1980

Black and Blue

Crossing the Styx

One-woman show at the Hudson River
  Museum, Yonkers, New York, organized by
  Richard Koshalek.

1981-82

Paper Puppets series

One-woman shows at the Butterworth Gallery,
  Hartford College, Hartford, Connecticut;
  the Terry Dintenfass Gallery, New York; and
  the Addison Ripley Gallery, Washington, D.C.

Returns to Sabah, Malaysia, to make documen-
  tary, *Borneo Playback; A Sabah Story*, 57
  minutes, in color.

Installing Paper Pillars, 1975.

1983

Receives grants from the Asia Foundation,
  the New York State Council on the Arts,
  and the National Endowment for the Arts.

1984

Named the first Distinguished Alumna of the
  University of Hartford Art School.

Ten-year retrospective exhibition at the Joseloff
  Gallery at the University of Hartford.

One-woman show at Loho Gallery, Louisville,
  Kentucky.

The artist in her studio with Paper Puppets, 1982

1985

Purdah

Borneo Playback aired on the Public
  Broadcasting System.

Attends show of Colombian sculptor Edgar
  Negret at Richard Humphrey's gallery, Fifth
  Street, New York. Begins a fruitful artist-
  dealer relationship with Humphrey that
  was to last ten years.

1986

Priestess

Priestess II

Sabah

Eloise and Abelard

Kadazan

One-woman show at the Humphrey Gallery,
  New York.

1988

Circle

Russ

Jefe

Jude

De Rapiña

Nara

One-woman shows at the two Humphrey
  Galleries, New York.

Shown at the ARCO International Art Fair,
  Madrid.

Richard Humphrey arranges travel to Spain in
  April to work at Fabrica Magisa on what
  would become the seven Spanish Bronzes.

1989

Erik the Red

Genji

1990

First Settler

Sheba (Queen of)

Ruth and Naomi

Samson

Potiphar's Wife

Indra

Kreeger Davidson with *Jude* at the Fabrica Magisa foundry in Madrid, 1988

The artist in her studio working on *Golem*, 1989

Kreeger Davidson with *Troy*, 1994

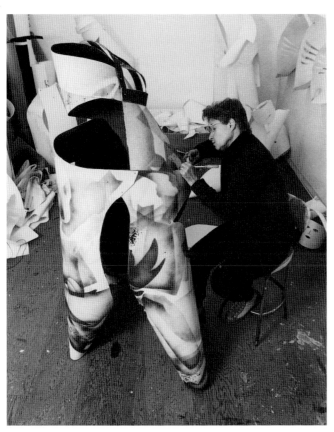

Kreeger Davidson with *Erik the Red* after its purchase by the Wadsworth Atheneum, 1989

1991
David Goliath
One-woman show at the Perimeter Gallery,
    Chicago.

1992
Sirens Sing
Euro-Apsaras
Upside Down and Sideways
J. C.
One-woman show at the Humphrey Gallery,
    New York.

1993
Inca/Nazca
One-woman show at the Perimeter Gallery,
    Chicago.

Visiting lecturer at the School of the Art
    Institute of Chicago.
One-woman show at the Mary and Leigh Block
    Museum of Art, Northwestern University,
    Evanston, Illinois.
Visiting lecturer at the Graduate School of
    Art, Theory, and Practice, Northwestern
    University.

1994
Medea
Troy
Helen and Paris
Soldiers
Cassandras
Markdowns
One-woman show at the Humphrey Gallery,
    New York.

Kreeger Davidson with *Sacella*, 1999

1995
Days of Danger series
One-woman show at Humphrey Pardo Gallery,
    New York.

1996
Designated Angels
One-woman show at the Humphrey Gallery,
    New York.
One-woman show at A.I.R. Gallery, New York.

1999
Sacella
One-woman show at the Babbidge Gallery,
    Storrs, Connecticut

2000
Reconstructed Issues

2001
Telamone

2002-03
Retrospective exhibition traveling to the
    Reading Public Museum, Reading,
    Pennsylvania; The National Museum of
    Women in the Arts, Washington, D.C.;
    New Britain Museum of American Art,
    New Britain, Connecticut.

ACKNOWLEDGMENTS

Chris Addison and Sylvia Riplex

Randy Alexander

Lawrence Alloway

Ted Behl

Carl Belz

Irving and Lois Blomstrann

Nanda Bonino

Judy Brown

Shu Leah Cheang

Garrett Congon

Dee Carnelli

Donald Davidson

Jim Dickens

Terry Dintenfass

Adam Eckstrom

Charles Ferguson

Sally Fisher

Muriel and Carl Fleishmann

Richard Foreman

Elizabeth Franck

Darlene and Tom Fridstein

Charles and Rose Gibbs

Bob Giza

Lloyd Glasson

Jim Gowan

Bernard Hanson

Brenda Huffman

Colleen Huffman

Richard Humphrey

Doug Hyland

Iron Clad Artists

Bethany Johns

Joan Kohn

Donald Kuspit

Chi Chin Liu

Jerry Lowengard

Babette Mangolte

Patrick McCaughy

Owen McNally

Robert P. Metzger

David Mickenberg

Cynthia Nadelman

Betty Parsons

Karen Peterson

Frank Pollack

The Pollowitz family

Denise Rene

Judith Roher

Ronald C. Roth

Dorothy Spear

Susan Fisher Sterling

Isabel Story

Jerry Thompson

Alan Tompkins

Peter Versteeg

John Weber

Sue Weil

Deborah Winkler

James Yood

Mary Ann Zeman and Mandy Macke

CONTRIBUTORS

ROBERT P. METZGER is Director Emeritus and Curator at the Reading Public Museum, Reading, Pennsylvania. As Director he was responsible for the restructuring and refurbishment of the museum and for building the permanent collection, especially in the areas of Asian, African, Oceanic, and twentieth-century art. The museum's new Twentieth Century Gallery houses works by Milton Avery, George Bellows, Pablo Picasso, Ruben Nakian, William Baziotes, Harry Bertoia, Ken Price, Sam Francis, Keith Haring, and many other important modern artists. Co-curating the Kreeger Davidson retrospective with Dr. Metzger is Richard Humphrey, with whom he collaborated on "Art and Technology," also at the Reading Public Museum.

DONALD KUSPIT is one of America's most respected art critics. Winner of the prestigious Frank Jewett Mather Award for Distinction in Art Criticism, Professor Kuspit is a contributing editor at *Artforum, Sculpture, New Art Examiner*, and *Tema Celeste* magazines, editor of *Art Criticism* and a member of the advisory board of *Centennial Review*.

CYNTHIA NADELMAN is an art critic, editor, and curator, as well as a poet. She has written on art for a variety of publications including *ARTnews*, where she is a contributing editor, *Drawing, American Heritage, Elle, Sulfur*, and numerous museum and gallery catalogues. Her poetry has been published in *The Paris Review, The Gettysburg Review, New American Writing, Denver Quarterly*, and *Partisan Review*.

SALLY FISHER worked in publications at the Metropolitan Museum of Art, New York, for over twenty years. She is the author of *The Square Halo*, published by Harry N. Abrams in 1995, as well as two children's books published by the Metropolitan Museum and Viking. Her poetry has appeared in *Field, New Directions, Chelsea, Poetry East, Shenandoah*, and many other magazines and anthologies.

PHOTOGRAPHY CREDITS